GUNA'S TRAVEL TO SATURN

A STORY WITH A RHYME, IN SPACE

SOUMYA V PADIPPURAKKAL

This is a work of fiction. All ideas expressed are of the author's. Name of real places have been mentioned to make the story interesting.

Grateful To God For This Book

He is a reader of your mind
With attention to all details
Glowing in gold and in black
With millions of lamps around
Be thankful, he is kind today
His fury, you won't be able to stand
Take some time to see him once
With some love and devotion
He will guide you then to the destination
One that was there in your mind
That he has seen from far off
Because he is God, the supreme power
With control of fortune and time
He is Krishna, Govinda, The Mahayogi

This book was possible by SreeGuruvayurappan's blessings.

Preface

Guna has been sent to Saturn
His travel, friends and return
That's what the book describes
Story is told just like a poem
So that it will create a rhyme
Rings on Saturn might not be same
But who knows, this might be real
Have fun while reading it
Please don't take it to the heart
Do let me know your opinion
It will make me feel good

- Soumya V Padippurakkal

Table of contents

Travel

'Where did I reach?' Guna was not sure
'What are these things?' he did wonder

Guna was startled, in turn alert
Turning around to face the colors

One's which flew, towards his face
Flying in air, with a pace

They were pebbles, in size of coins
Moving at a meter, above the ground

It looked like they were on a travel
Running parallel, at a fixed level

Each had a colour, different to other
They did move, close to one another

Crimson, blue, yellow and silver
Green and brown were also seen

Pebbles had a glow, on their surface
As if glitter, applied to their face

It took some time for Guna to realize
That pebbles were polite, also nice

As if they knew Guna was there
Pebbles did bend, just around him

They repelled, as if to a magnet
Whose like pole had come near them

Some went left, some towards right
Increasing their speed, with each step

They had a sensor that was sure
Changing the path as Guna went near

'What's wrong with you?' Guna did tell
As if the objects could hear him well

Solitude does make people speak
To themselves or to that unknown

Guna couldn't be blamed for it
This place was quite new to him

Pebbles were not at fault, of course
They were flexible, like before

Making space for this new being
Whom they call as human being

They are seen once in a while
When their craft gets pulled down

*'They come to see our beautiful land
Guests they are,'* that's what was told

****

Land looked bright , also green
Guna walked and ran on that land

There were bushes, rocks and flies
Flowers and trees, looked with delight

For half a day, did Guna run
He reached a cliff top, with a view

It was a valley, seen below
One that was wide , lying low

Guna climbed down the cliff
To reach that valley, seen as an ocean

Not with water, but with pebbles
Enormous were they, in number

'Together they looked blue in colour'
Or was it Guna's imagination!

Pebbles did go towards the right
Trees were there, to their left

Guna took the path on left
Seeing some green, at a height

He walked towards them in a hurry
With a belief to find friends many

'Journey afar would be a joyous one
That's what he had thought like a dream'

Guna felt, he heard that song
He listened, to find the singer

It was a bird, who flew ahead
With her head, turned around

The bird was happy to see Guna
'A new listener to her songs '

She turned her head again and again
To check if Guna was indeed coming

Of course, he was coming to the orchard
The one filled with pink orchids

The bird had skin, green in colour
With a twisted beak which was red

Her shape was that of a Koel bird
So was the sweetness of her voice

Her feathers were long and round
Wide as well for her to glide

Guna walked slowly amongst the plants
So as to leave the flowers intact

As the orchids swayed with wind
Guna felt they had their own face

With a pair of eyes and nose
There was a smile, on their lips

The bird was flying ahead of Guna
Her mind and sound moving with time

She had flown on to a man's shoulder
Who was tall with shoulders broad

'Krishna is the name' said the man
As Guna reached the log near him

'Have some water, you are tired'
He gave Guna a full tumbler

The man looked familiar, even human
Realized Guna as the water was half

'Where did the pebbles go to?' asked Guna
'Even I have no idea' said the man

'Well, I'm not sure if The Bird knows '
Said he, after a little pause

'Come, come 'We've a long way to go '
Krishna walked in front of Guna

They walked beside the pink flowers
Flourishing in the garden green

The Bird kept her music alive
Soon the Sun appeared in the sky

'Where are we walking to?' asked Guna
'To where The bird decides' said Krishna

The Bird felt proud, of the trust in her
Shown by Krishna, like none other

But she was not sure of the way ahead
As it was different every other time

They will find the land one day
The one golden with lots of men

That's what she had learnt in time
It will be seen to earnest one's

'What will I do then?'
That's what The bird didn't know

Trees

Guna felt it was a desert in front
It looked fierce, with grains of sand

It must have been a mile and half
Since they met the sand, on their path

A coating was formed, on their face
Glasses did keep their eyes safe

The Bird stood still, as if on a hill
That's what it felt from there

She was sitting on a branch, not on air
It being visible, once they went near

The branch was thin, tall as well
It had colour of brown and yellow

Branches were long, many in number
On that tree, where The bird did wait

The tree was not one to be alone
It had friends that spread all around

Similar in colour, with no marks found
Smooth and proud, did they stand

There must've been a forest once
View of trees was one of that

It must've been a long time ago
Colour of leaves was now same as land

Not many leaves, were to be found
On the trees, standing on ground

Nor could they be seen below
On the land, which was yellow

Perhaps they dried in the heat for long
Forming the sand, that's lying down

A sound was heard, from above
It was The Bird, hitting on a branch

Checking the quality, of that wood
Perhaps to see, if it's edible or not

'You are no woodpecker', said Krishna
To The Bird who knew better

Trees could provide, no shade at all
None was there for them as well

The men walked beside the trees
Holding the trunk, sliding them back

Walk was slow, as path was crowded
With those roots, as long as the branches

Arched as a bow, at some places
Going deep in to earth, at other instance

It looked similar to human veins
Protruding out from skin on the arms

Disappearing to a place way inside
Just when it nears, the finger tips

Branches leaned to either side
Perhaps trying to put a word across

To the nearest neighbor that they had
Which was a tree, who stood nearby

The Bird jumped from branch to branch
Showing the way, that was seen ahead

Guna and Krishna could only walk
The Bird wished that they could fly

'If they had wings just like me
We could have reached, far from here
But wings were given only to me,
I'm the one who can fly and how!
It's my duty to show the way
Watching the sky and pathway
If I had wings like the eagle
I could fly high and fast
God made my wings little small
So that I'll go slow as a snail
It gives me time to think ahead
Unlike the one's, who think alike
I feel so special this time of day
Just like how I always do
Before the Sun sets, we need to act
So that the heat doesn't get to us '

The bird sang loud, pretty clear
As she flew with a confident smile

That's when a wind, touched her face
It was cold, because of moisture

The Bird shook her skin, with vigour
Wind did give her a cold vibe

Now she searched for water below
That was the message from that wind

'Did I indeed feel the cold
Or was it just the air around?'

Then she heard the familiar sound
One which soothes the restless mind

Of the wind moving with a rhythm
Being in love with the flowing river

Becoming calm, by its presence
Trying to be cold, in the process

The Bird spread her wings wide
Gliding towards a river ahead

River was still, like the surroundings
Hard to decipher, if it was flowing

As The Bird took a dip in the river
Her green feathers turned to brown

Water was flowing, below the surface
Mud was filled, as a layer above

The Bird had to flutter inside the water
That's when Guna could see it clear

'Indeed it's water down there'
Exclaimed Guna as he took a handful

'In spite of water running beside
Why do the trees, have less leaves'

Krishna was lost, with that thought
Pondering on it, he stayed quite

'We need to think of a way ahead
To walk beside or to go across' said Guna

They walked along, through the woods
Trying to find, something there

With no plan on what it was
They were on a random walk

River beside was still in brown
Mud above could clearly be seen

As their eyes wandered far
Waves could be seen far away

Seen as a few highs and lows
It did look like river did flow

Now they knew one thing for sure
Way ahead is through river itself

Tunnel

'A ship cannot be built right now'
Guna and Krishna were practical

'But we can make a small boat
With the woods, from these trees

Few branches will have to be cut
A strong canoe can then be built'

Krishna had the tools, so did Guna
They opened the bag, one on their back

It had an axe, folded to be compact
Which did open, with a unique code

Now the axe was a meter in length
Being ready to cut some wood

Branches were up, touching the skies
Guna and Krishna climbed the trees

Though they looked petite and thin
The wood had become thick skinned

For more than a thousand one years
Did they stand, in this heat

Guna and Krishna cut the branches
Sweating a lot, in the process

They searched around, for the one's
Which were perfect for their purpose

Logs were made smooth and even
It was tied with nylon strings

To form a strong canoe
Light in weight, for them to float

'These tools will come useful for you
Iris had told me before I started

How did she know?' Krishna wondered
'Who's Iris?' Guna had to enquire
'She's the one who gave you that '
He pointed to the axe in Guna's hands

'Diana gave it to me' Guna was sure
Krishna just shrugged, left to right

'It's all the same, Diana or Iris
They are a few brains, put to use
They think it can be solved in time

It's not easy, as they think
Creators are more creative than them
It won't be realized, any time soon
Axe and the strings were put to use
Of course they know more than us
Not all they know, that's for sure
Else, why would we be sent again?'

Guna agreed, so did The Bird
They placed the canoe, on the mud

It didn't float in the river ahead
Getting stuck near the banks itself

Canoe was pushed for some momentum
It didn't budge, not even a bit

'Is there no flow for this river?'
Guna had a doubt, seeing it still

'It does have' Krishna was confident
'Don't you see the waves out there?
Mud below is holding it back
Tons of force, will have to be applied '

As they slide the mud to the side

Canoe did move, with a new life

It then floated away from those trees
Towards the waves, seen in the river

The bird sat on Krishna's shoulder
She looked ahead, from the canoe's rear

Guna sat on the other edge
Trying to row or go with the flow

It must've been a couple of minutes
They did admire the surrounding water

Canoe increased its speed with the river
Which was flowing, fast than before

Everyone was scared, to the core
It made them look up above

Canoe did dip at Krishna's side
As Guna tried to balance them all

The bird thought it was the end
Everyone else did think the same

She was wrong, as they were sliding
Down and down, to a place unknown

Canoe was slanting, just like before
Speed and angle, remaining as prior

They had entered a moving passage
In that darkness, there was silence

Water was not around, that was sure
They could breathe, like before

'What just happened?' asked Guna
'We're alive ' exclaimed Krishna
*'I just know that the canoe slipped
Somewhere in the middle of the river'*

It would have been boring and scary
If not for the The bird's songs

The bird closed her eyes, playing a tune
Remembering her partner back home

Whose feathers were brown,
Stripes below his chest, had a shine

'How we used to play in the river
Trying to get some fishes from there
Little did I know, journey was far
That we were going, miles apart
I had lost hope of a return
That's when Guna, came to town
His suit was same as what Krishna had
Even the bag did look similar
It's been a day, since we backpacked
Now I'm hopeful about our future '

The bird's songs relaxed her mind
So did it help the men as well

It felt like many years had gone
It was in fact more than an hour

'Light can be seen far ahead,' said Guna
'Colours are there, seen like stars '

The bird opened her eyes with a smile
Her smile faded within an instant

As they were moving down itself
But speed of the canoe had reduced

Light was there, seen down the line
Canoe had changed its angle now

It was more aligned to the ground
Then it stopped, coming to a halt

They had reached the unique land
One which came at the tunnel's end

As the canoe had stopped to move
Guna and Krishna started to walk

They walked towards a feeble light
One seen on the farther side

Golden Slide

Cold it was, more than usual
Ice it was, seen very clear

Like mountains and towers did it stand
Few other shapes could also be seen

Guna felt dizzy , he clenched his teeth
The Bird didn't move, as she sneezed

'Is it a city there in front?'
They did wonder, with hope of a life

Guna and Krishna had spacesuits
It was special, with a knob on the side

They could adjust the temperature
One inside the suits, they wore

They turned the knob, to the side
It kept them warm, from inside

The bird didn't care, she was bold
Ice won't freeze her, she was sure

'So thick is my feather
As if it's made of leather

Ice and fire, can't touch me ever
It has become tough, as the aim is now near'

Suit could only adjust the body
Flakes that flew was not yet planned

Tiny granules flying from ice
Rose like embers from the fire

It flew to them from all the sides
Like a storm it hit their eyes

Krishna was now concerned
He made it obvious through his words

'I waited for months, in the woods
Then I heard the bird's songs
As we travelled, seeing the places
That's when Guna came along
It made me aware, I'm still alive
My limited mortality is still in place
Happy, hopeful ,alive I became
Walking and dancing on this land
But this place looks a bit plain
Can it be due to absence of plants?'

Guna was having a similar concern
He echoed same thought, as his friend

'We did sing, we did laugh
Land did change, as we walked
It had colours, shapes and life
With sound of birds and the wind
Now we stand, on the land of ice
One that comes at the end of tunnel'

Sun was bright ,with his light
From some place far off in the night

A beacon of hope it was to the men
Darkness is far, that's what it meant

'We've to leave this land behind'
That's what they were sure about

They bend down on the ground
Keeping the bird close to heart

They crawled ahead with all their might
Towards a peak, covered in snow

As a wind blew with force

Ice on the peak, withered to the side

Only a stump, remained now
Of the hill, which once stood tall

Off they went, towards that stump
Which was just a meter in height

Flakes of ice, still danced around
As they walked around the stump

It looked hollow, beneath the surface
Krishna bent down, to get a glance

A heap of ice, moved over them
Guna was happy to arise again

Krishna was not to be seen anywhere
He had slipped, near the stump

Guna and The bird, watched from above
As their friend, roared out loud

He was sliding on a golden round
It went in a circle wide and long

It felt like a crater, was down there
Which had lines, golden in colour

The bird was quick, like her voice
She flew ahead, to meet her friend

Ice was there, still on the land
It didn't enter, the golden slide

'There was no friction on that path'
Guna realized, as he joined them

'Golden colour is just an illusion
Real gold is a known tradition
You will see them on all and how
As you reach down in the land
People there will be walking ahead
Their search will never end '

The bird spoke, just for her ears
With a bright smile, in her eyes

There was little that she could tell
They had to figure it, on their own

Of course not a thing they knew

Of what she saw in the land below

Shoulder to shoulder did she fly
From Guna to Krishna and back again

The slide was taking them along
It had a movement of its own

There were lines, seen a bit light
It was a path, etched crisp and precise

They had to slide on those lines
It took them along, as it went right

Down an inch, with each minute gone
They were off, to some far off land

Guna raised his head upwards
To see the ice, with his eyes

Ice couldn't be seen, even far off
Sky was seen as a blue round above

As they spiraled, down and round
They did feel a spin on the head

Distance from above did reduce
As the space in front became narrow

Guna was the one to observe it first
The area decreased, along with depth

It looked small, like a vowel
To where it goes, it was a puzzle

Speed was stable, to begin with
Then it increased, for a while.

People

'Hope you are there' said Krishna
As he went ahead of Guna

'One thing you cannot take from me
That's my wits, my dear friend
I used to tell, when in a circle
Too proud , being that naïve
It kept me going, day or night
Anyone along with me or not'

Said Guna, he was not ready for this
Even the wits couldn't help him now

Guna had a sensor, in his hand
Embedded deep, into his suit

Sensor was tethered, to the spacecraft
Just that there were no ropes used

Spacecraft was the one, he had taken
For his travel, to this far off land

It did show the way back to craft
Once he walked, around or away.

Since the plunge on the colour pebbles

The sensor had lost a bolt somewhere

Busy was Guna, to observe the absence
Of the only thing, which was present

It was the thing for Guna to know
If he was ever going back home

All of a sudden, there was a flashlight
From the sensor who was silent

It meant that the craft was near
Guna's eyes was filled with tears

He tapped on the sensor, in return
There was no display, like before

He kept on trying, to make it work
Till he fell, from the golden slide

Guna was busy, tilting his arms
He didn't realize, change in land

On the edge of the slide they stood
With their feet, standing on ground

'Can we travel back, defying gravity?'
Krishna asked, looking up at the slide

'It's not possible ' He did conclude
That's when Guna looked around

They were on a land, which was golden
It did spread wide, like an ocean

The bird was chill, as she knew
She had seen it, when it was new

During the trip, she made before
That was almost a decade ago

'Didn't I tell you of the gold there
You will see it on people there
Down in the land, which is real
It depends on your luck as well '

The bird spoke, just like before
None could understand, as always

A few men walked past, in a hurry
They didn't stop, to smile or listen

They went by, without a noise
From a distance, they looked fierce

'Who are these men?' Krishna was alert
Eager to tell them, reason for their visit

Three men stopped, turned and smiled
They stood ahead, as if in thought

They smiled seeing, Guna and Krishna
Of course the little bird, looked familiar

They were not alone, those three men
Many did walk, in front of them

They had a couple of hands and legs
Fingers on them, long and sharp

It felt like made of molten gold
Hands and feet, curved at the ankles

Red was the border, of their eyes
Inside was a pupil, black and thin

Their face was round, perfect in shape
Lips in place, below the nose

Red it looked, to the human eyes
It curved a bit, as they smiled

Covered in gold, from head to waist
A golden envelope, till their knees

Their hands looked yellow in colour
Same as what was seen on the feet

*'People were same, but for their hands
It was strong, just like iron '*

Guna realized, as he shook hands
With those men, who had come

The three men had now come near
Trying to have some friendly talk

'Hey hey man,' they cheered a bit
'Aren't you from earth?' they asked

Guna's eyes widened, on hearing that
Realization struck, he's not on earth

Far off he was, in the land of Saturn
One which is known, for no return

'Did I really make the trip? asked Guna
'Of course, we did ' Krishna was certain

Saturn

Some said the colour was red
Others thought it was a bit black

Golden it looked, none knew it still
Many did search, till their time

There were no roads, nor any trees
It was just yellow metal seen around

Air was golden, so was the land
People wore gold, so did the kittens

They were all walking, to where?
Perhaps even they didn't know

There was no water, or any green
But a golden colour, till the eyes met

Far ahead, land did rise in height
'Perhaps a hill' Guna assumed

Even that was golden, tall and bright
A red coloured glow was on its peak

People there looked very similar
To humans, who had gone from earth

'Walk along , you cannot stop '
Said the three men, who had stopped

'Can you see us?' asked Guna
'Of course, is that even a question?
You are tall, black eyes and handsome
Looking tried, perhaps of the travel
One along with you, looks a bit mushy
His beard is long, so is his hair
The bag he carries, is bigger than him
There is nothing to take in it
Green coloured bird, flying above
Has long feathers and a twisted beak'

The men knew well, they smiled
It looked like that as the lips widened

Guna was sure that the men could see
'To where are you going?' asked Guna

'To the tree, where we will take some rest '
Said the men as they walked

Krishna was equally confused
But he didn't beat an eyelid,

He knew this was to come
It was told, before he even started

Wait was over, as a tree approached
As tall as Guna, but a bit thin

It's trunk was golden, same as branches
Only a single leaf did it have

Leaf was green, small as well
Standing above on the tallest branch

Everyone lay down, around the tree
On the ground, near its trunk

Like the leaves, that would have fallen
Once, when it was beautiful and green

'Time to sleep,' said the man nearby
Guna and Krishna agreed with a shrug

'Are they even human?' asked Guna
'Of course we are,' said one of them
'Lure for wealth brought us here
A long time ago, before you were born
Our eyes are red, because of greed

Still we collect, more than the need
We keep the gold, which we wear
Then we walk, till the next tree
Generous are we, to all who come
To share is divine, that's what we believe
The light you see, at a height
Far off in the land of night
That's the one, with one red leaf
Only one seen in this world
Now we've to walk till there
We've heard it's one of a kind
It's bright and hot, if you get there
Still we try, to reach beyond
Fools we are and price we pay
Enough of stories, it's time to sleep '

Said the man, all of a sudden
As he went to get some sleep

Guna and Krishna looked at each other
As if they were the only people there

It had taken them, quarter of an hour
To reach this tree, that was near

They did drink, some pure water

The one they carried in the bag

A man in gold just gave a smile
As he was offered water to drink

'Thank you ,but no thank you' said he
'Let me know if you have some tea'

As everyone slept in an instant
Krishna raised his head, his eyes wide

He wanted to see, the view in front
Of those people, with the tree beside

As he observed the people there
They looked familiar to him by now

There were three twenty one of them
In the group, seen ahead

Their eyes were open, like before
Perhaps they slept, like horses do

Nobody moved an inch to the side
Still like a statue, crafted with clay

Statue does smile, after a while
If you look, long in its eyes

Perhaps it can be the life inside
Who has heard the surrounding words

The men here didn't have that smile
They looked plain, like a glass crystal

That's when Krishna realized the fact
There were no women in that group

****

In year seventy five, did they go first
To see those planets, lying in space

Man made the search, far and wide
In that world, beyond the earth

Not for answers for this creation
But for life, that's there in common

He did find, many a mysteries
Some did fade, like fine stories

A trick that was played by nature
To protect the beings, she nurtures

'Saturn was safe, from all sides
It can be seen, even in shades
A walk uphill, with those men
Is sure to be a lesson for them'

That's what nature had in her mind
She did allow, the travel beyond

Attraction

It looked the one most unreal
None could tell, what's real there

'Elements are abundant, useful for all'
That's what spread like a wildfire

Of the area, that was never seen
Told in folktales and in dreams

Until man made that move
One expected from him too

Time and again, people did travel
With lots of food and some tools

In search of a planet different to theirs
That was until, one of them returned

'Mr. Flint' was his name, an ocean scientist
He was the one who came back, again

'They are alive, that I'm sure'
Said Mr. Flint, about his teammates
'On a walk, with one's found afar
They did chose, to stay back there

It took me a year, to go around
Seeing it all, to get many details
One's which were left behind itself
As a gratitude to the friends I made
People are nice, they have gold
They walk a lot, in many groups'

That's all what Mr. Flint had told
Before disappearing into some zone

To where he went, not many knew
'He was tired', that's what was told

Mr. Flint had gone to live in silence
To some place, to find some solace

Journey he had was a beautiful one
With friends and birds, lakes and hills

He did have a picture in mind
Visuals of which had no sound

That's how it was felt from there
Portrait it was, spread very rare

Though it was a pleasant stay

Mr. Flint vowed to stay away

After a decade since that mission
One which brought him, back to earth

A scientist was sent again to Saturn
Who was an expert, just in oceans

Expectation of a miracle, as like before
But with some data, unlike prior

His name was Guna, a happy soul
Who loved nature and its beings

A hundred years did it feel
To those eyes, that seen things real

Into the realms of an oceanic view
With waves like streams plenty to see

Mission was one beyond the mind
Not to think is what was wise

Still Guna did, as he was new
Not to mention others who knew

After a month, since he started
In search of the planet, called Saturn

That stays far away from the Sun
Perhaps with people, one of its own

Guna saw a multitude of colours
Lying random, shining like mirrors

He lowered his craft, to get a view
Of that area, which looked different

That's all what he remembered now
Spacecraft had gone down, like a paper

Though the landing was hard
Craft was intact, making Guna glad

Destination was right, per coordinates
But contact was lost, with earth

Guna opened the doors, of the airlock
Being careful to close the door tight

He came outside, to see the land
One on which his spacecraft did stand

Guna had a spacesuit, with a helmet
It was meant to protect him there

Suit had oxygen, for him to breathe
Water was there, to quench the thirst

He found it tough to walk like that
Coming on toes, at times on knees

Surprised he was, by the impact
The helmet was raised, just to check

There was air, fresh like before
Normal he felt, like on earth

'Is this not Saturn?' Guna was not sure
He made his mind, to explore the land

There were particles that flew around
Colourful one's, seen from above

Guna had walked, along with them
They were the pebbles, one's with glitter

Who did fly, above the ground
Towards the valley, below the cliff

Guna had met The bird there
With her songs and a friendly smile,

She had taken him to Krishna's side
Amongst those orchids with the face

Guna and Krishna had walked along
To reach the river with many trees.

Canoe was built, using the tools
It had slipped, in the midst of river

They had seen the slide and ice
Before reaching this golden land

Now Guna lay beside the tree
One standing alone with a single leaf

He did sleep for the first time
Since he came to this new planet

****

As it was dawn, land shone bright
Men still slept, as if it was night

Guna was awakened, by a sparrow
She spoke very close to his ears

Her beaks kept moving, making a sound
Continuous it was, not willing to stop

Sparrows

Sparrow's eyes were black and round
It looked like a mirror, for those around

The beak was tiny, shaped like rainbow
They were shining, along with the Sun

Yellow was its colour, like her feet
Her skin was brown, same as feathers

'What happened?' Guna asked confused
Sparrow just stared, into his eyes

The bird was surprised to see a sparrow
Who was smaller, than her nose

Krishna was asleep, with some dreams
The bird nudged him, with her beak

He woke up with two sleepy eyes
Startled to see a sparrow in front

Krishna and Guna got up to check
Then the sparrow rose from the ground

As she flew, they followed her trail
They were in for some surprise

Land around still had that glow
Like that of a bride, with her bow

Men wearing gold, slept peacefully
They didn't see the sparrow fly

As Krishna and Guna walked till a turn
They were joined, by fellow sparrows

Not in hundreds or in thousands
They saw a swarm of flying birds

Their number was beyond a count
Flying ahead, with a deafening sound

All the sparrows were coloured brown
They were a force, looking strong

They flew fast and close together
With not an inch of space in between

Path ahead was not to be seen
They did wish, that it was green

The bird was happy to see the sparrows
She sat safe, on Krishna's shoulder

They had walked a mile and half
Since the golden tree, with leaf

Where those men, might still be there
Preparing for the journey together

Guna did search for the little one
Who had come to wake him up

Sparrow was not found or recogonized
As all of them looked the same

A few of them, flew sideways
Away from the fleet, making a way

Ahead of them, sat few others
On a thing, which looked familiar

'Oh my God' , Guna's tears started to fall
As he stood, trusting in faith

As the sparrows rose above them
A spacecraft was seen on that land

Not any craft was it, you see !
It was the one, from the earth

One on which, Guna had come
A couple of days, before today

Flag on its wings, hardly visible
Logo on the front, was clear to all

'Did you come in this?' asked Krishna
'Yes I did' Guna looked around
'It's the spacecraft that took me here
One which I left, few days back
The place was not this, that's for sure
There were flying pebbles, I saw
This golden land here is unique
I have not seen it, before this day
How did the craft land up here
Can the sparrows, lift its weight?'

Guna was confused by the thought
'They can't ' Krishna was sure

A few sparrows still sat on the craft
Sparrows on the craft continued to chirp

'Why do these men, still stand here?'
Wondered the sparrows, in unison

They flew around, round and round
Till the head, started to spin

Not of theirs, but of The Bird's
She was lost, in her own thoughts

'Indeed, it's a spacecraft in front
It's not the one in which I had come
Mine had a blue tail, not yellow
Even Logo looks different from mine
If at all this belongs to earth
Should I travel back in it?
It's been a decade, since I left home
My partner would have gone by now
Even the kids would have grown and left
Their offspring's won't accept me now
There is no one waiting for me
Then why should I even go back to earth
Perhaps I'm immortal in this land
Helping all who come to work
I know this place by heart by now
Of course there is left to explore
Will these sparrows take me in?
Into their fleet, which is so huge
I would be an asset to them, for sure
Only if they knew, about my skills

None of them can sing like me
Nor can they travel, for so long
I should set up a meeting with them
Before they disappear, into their zone '

The bird fluttered, her wings fast
Making a rumble, never heard from her
'Don't be scared, we will be safe inside'
Guna tried to console the bird

She wouldn't listen to any of it
Having decided in her mind

Her wings were flapping, up and down
The eyes did have a drop of tear

Krishna felt he understood her
They have been friends, for quite long

'Let her stay back, it's better for her'
He kept an affectionate hand on The
Bird

As the men agreed with her
That's when The bird relaxed a bit

Flying back and forth between them
Trying to give a good farewell

Then she flew out, to the air
Not to turn back and see the craft

Voice of sparrows, millions in count
Could be heard, from somewhere near

Perhaps they stood keeping a watch
On that man , friend of The bird

Who was different, from the others
With no care, of the gold they had

Or of the life that he could have had
That's only if he wished he had

The Bird's Song

Guna and Krishna walked around
To check the craft, for the travel back

Multiple compartments were opened
Then they stood inside a vacuum

Guna stepped in, with a long breath
A smile on his face, seeing all intact

The controls, switches, lights in cockpit
Brakes, panes, sensors and electronics

They all looked same as before
Smiling back at their friend Guna

Spacecraft was larger than liberty
Still space they had was compact

Just enough to fit them both
And the control panel, in front

*'Sparrows did try to get inside
To turn me left and to the right
They couldn't enter, due to the airlock
Which was metallic and tightly locked'*

Guna felt he heard those words
From the mike, who stood close

Guna and Krishna got ready for travel
They wore the suits which were special

A green coloured knob was pressed
It was for the spacecraft to launch

They had to gain a high speed
So as to leave Saturn's gravity

Rocket engines had to be powered
One's kept at the rear of the craft

Which were fueled by radio isotopes
It was a new experiment tried by man

Guna and Krishna waited for an hour
Then the spacecraft started to drift

As the craft rose, Guna saw the men
One's with two red coloured eyes

Those who had gold, from head to toe
Who walked in search of the golden tree

They were on the land, looking fierce
Walking ahead, towards the trees

They didn't look up, to check the sound
One created by Guna's spacecraft

Guna could see next stop of the men
It was a tree, with a single leaf

Tree looked near, from up above
A day is what it will take in real

Trees were there at equal distance
Kept in place, as if by chance

Group of sparrows, were seen on them
It looked like they had their own city

Ahead of them, ice was there
Spread like mountain, beyond their land

Trees were seen, till the ice
'Do the men know this fact?'

Guna and Krishna searched below
For The Bird, who might be there

Krishna felt he saw a tinge of green
'That's The bird there' he told in vain

She looked different and colourful
Unlike the sparrows brown and small

The bird did turn her head and see
On hearing the sound of the craft

She decided to sing her words
As she always did with her thoughts

'Guna and Krishna were new to Saturn
Of the ice and gold, pebbles and wood
One's who send them, the people on earth
This place is not alien to them
Many of theirs have come here before
They are no fools, that's so sure
In spite of it not being fruitful
Still the people continue to come
What do they search- the unknown
It's never to be found- it's so known
I would love to tell them this
But my language is way too different
One billion miles is the distance
A month is what it used to take

A decade ago, when I did come
Now it's faster, that's what I heard
A few did go till the golden land
They couldn't find their craft there
Except for these two gentlemen here
Fiery Krishna and the humble Guna
I'm happy, for both of them
As they are going to see their own
Guna was the one who was lucky
To find his craft in two days
How it happened? Will remain a mystery
Perhaps the sparrows know the story
They might tell it to me as well
During the night, when we will rest.'

There was no sadness or a tear
As The bird felt it all in vain

She was now part of a bigger group
One of sparrows who did speak

Sparrows were busy in their task
To realize someone was missing

It was the tiniest of them all
Who loved adventures and some risk

****

Spacecraft did go in an imaginary path
Spherical it was, close to the ground

Guna now saw the view so proper
With land of golden men, at the centre

Ice did spread, around the land
With the slide, seen as a border

The one which had very thin lines
On which Guna and Krishna did slide

There was a river, around the ice
Standing like a snake, coiled in shape

River was not brown as it had been
Mud beside was not to be seen

It had waves and tides flowing along
In bright colours of purple and blue

Water and ice mixed so perfect
Tunnel below was not to be found

The one on which canoe did glide
As it connected to the land of ice

'Where is the tunnel?' wondered the men
Hidden it was from their eyes

On the river shores, stood the trees
One's with a few yellow leaves

They looked rusty, tired as well
Giant and wide, with many branches

It felt like sand spread on the ground
They were in fact roots of the trees

Number of trees was beyond a count
Something that they never realized.

Rings

Just around those endless trees
Multitude of colours could be seen

Guna felt his head was spinning
Not by the move, but by the view

Of those colourful pebbles seen
Flying above the land, which was green

Glitter was there on their surface
Shining like stars were those objects

They glided from a point to other
Taking along the wind with them

'That's where my spacecraft had landed'
Said Guna, pointing to the land below

Krishna did see the pebbles there
He found it tough, to believe the story

All of a sudden, they began to shake
Craft was being pulled to the ground

Just like it happened a while ago
As Guna had entered inside Saturn

'No, no not again' said Guna
Now more experienced, than before

He gave more force for acceleration
Then the craft went high and higher

Guna glanced at the land below
Searching amongst the flying pebbles

To see that force, attracting the craft
Away from the path towards home

Though that force couldn't be found
Land looked familiar and nostalgic

'Didn't we just see this land?' said a voice
That was of Krishna, from beside

'Exactly, that's what even I wondered'
Said Guna, seeing the men below

The land, one with gold was seen again
Very near to the flying pebbles

It still had those men, walking on it
They did go from tree to tree

Sparrows did sit on a bunch of branches
Eagerly waiting for those men

Ice was there, beyond the gold
So was seen, the river in brown

Trees with branches, long and thin
Stood beside with bow like roots

Tunnel in dark and golden slide
All were seen close behind

It was a sight, beyond their mind
Seeing the same land, again and again

Spacecraft moved in a spiral path
To gain momentum and the speed

Guna was in awe of the land below
One's which looked, as seen before

He felt that they were in a loop
Being visible with moving time

It was a ring, Guna realized
Each with layers, seven in number

Three twenty two, was the count
Of the rings, which existed there

They repeated around each other
With their contents being similar

Guna had just been to the first
Remaining stood away from the middle

Vastness of rings was beyond limits
Its area kept increasing with distance

His craft would rise, then it would fall
Whenever the layer of pebbles appeared

'Can it be gravity?' wondered Guna
As he flew away from them

Guna did see a few yellow ships
They were seen in the land of pebbles

There was no trace of anyone there
Except for the orchids with the face

Guna kept wondering on his luck
How the craft was found so quick

Men covered in gold didn't hear a thing
Looking forward to only their goal

Though he had moved far from there
It looked like the land did come near

Ground level increased with each layer
It felt like they were still in there

Guna was determined to steer ahead
With all his might and of the craft's

More pebbles were seen flowing
Where it marked planets boundary

Spacecraft now rose at a right angle
As Guna felt it was the thing right

Off they went till they could
Until the pebbles could not be seen

Then they moved away to a cloud
Which did feel like showing the way

Cloud was a bit blue and black
Part of a cluster that was behind

They were circling the planet
On their way to a place nearby

Guna took his craft a bit to the left
Making it parallel to those clouds

Then it travelled away from the land
One which was trying to pull it back

Colour of layers was not to be seen
Nor was there sign of land

It felt like clouds that spread around
Enveloped the planet as a whole

Guna did feel sad for a while
Leaving the land beautiful behind

A familiar voice was then heard
Guna searched for the source of sound

It was the sparrow brown in colour
One who woke them up at dawn

Now she sat on the panel in front
Making a sound that was still the same

Little sparrow walked from left to right
With many switches, monitors beside

Guest on the Craft

Beak of the sparrow was very active
It was pressing on different colours

The one seen on one of the keyboards
It felt like he would pluck them up

'Should we open the doors?'
Guna and Krishna stood confused

They were not sure how it entered
Nor they knew how far they were

With no idea of what was to be done
About this guest who looked restless

They did evaluate all the options
Going back was never opted

As they were far away from Saturn
And the sparrow fleet that flew

'She would never make it on her own
To the golden home that sparrows have
It would be foolish on our part
To risk our lives and of the sparrow's
How did you get inside of this?'

They asked the little sparrow

Guna kept an eye on the sparrow
Who was talking a lot about something

He had a voice loud and clear
It was just different from men on earth

Neither Guna nor Krishna understood
But they listened as he was special

Sparrow was silent for a while
As he observed the view outside

He had decided it a while ago
Since a year that had gone by

That he wanted to travel to earth
In one of the crafts which will be there

'I want to see that land unique
About which our forefathers speak
One with green trees and plants
With fruits on them to eat a lot
Where there is water everywhere
In ocean, rivers, lakes and ponds

Human beings walk hand in hand
With animals, mammals, also birds
There are forts, caves and temples
Which are unique, wonder to the eyes
Places are there, beautiful are they
A lifetime it will take to see them all
Let me go with one of them
Who will take me as their own'

Sparrow's demand was not accepted
By her tribe who were protective

'It's not safe for you, little one
They might harm you being polite'

Elders tried to advice him in vain
Sparrow was adamant in his wish

When he saw Guna and Krishna
Them being friends with The Bird

The one in green who also sings
Sparrow did make his mind strong

To go with them on their spacecraft
On a trip to the land called earth

One of which he had heard a lot
And wished to see with his eyes

He had got in through a valve
Which did flap at the rear of craft

Silent was he for all this while
Else the men would have left him back

With his group, in the land of gold
They would be sure, it was best for him

Sparrow wanted to realize his dream
Which was to see the earth in whole

Now he raised one leg sideways
Bending his beak to the front

As he did his own sparrow yoga
Came a smile on his face and the men's

There were objects flying past
Some were slow others a bit fast

All of them had a different light
As they went past, they did shine bright

'Is it their own or the Sun's?'
There was no answer to that yet

It looked they would hit in space
But for Guna's craft expertise

Clouds around still remained there
Though it was more than an hour

They were dark as if it will rain
But after few hours, it turned plain

As they moved away to the sides
Space ahead, was then clearly seen

Milky Way it was, showing the way
With roads and lights along the way

Silence is what, space sounds like
That's what they heard all this while

But lots of sound could be heard
Some like thunder, that too fierce

'One at a time, will we sleep
Sparrow shouldn't feel alone'

That's the decision that they made
For sparrow was special and a guest

Guna rolled into his colorful bed
Where he slept with his eyes closed

Floating above in that little space
The place for him to sleep in outer space

Krishna decided to guard the sparrow
Till the time that Guna slept

Little sparrow on the control panel
Reminded him of his friend, The Bird

'Once in a lifetime you get friends
Like The bird ,selfless and polite
Who did ensure that I returned safe
While she decided to stay back
She had brought me cherries often
From where it came, it was not known
Sitting on a branch singing a song
She had shown the way for long
Until Guna had come along
With the hopeful smile that he had'

Once in a while he saw peacocks
Who moved together with their folks

Krishna had to double tap his hand
So as not to be dreaming again.

Happiness

Guna had a concern, he woke up
Worried he was about the guest.

'Little sparrow is not safe on earth
People there are not that right
I know pretty well, about my friends
The one's who search for new elements
They might see him just as an object
For them to do scientific research
We need to protect the sparrow from them
Till the time he finds a place
Our team on earth would have known
That I am not coming back alone
Movements would have been read
Of not just one but of the three'

Krishna did agree with the thought
'But how?' that's what he didn't know

'One week is what it will take
To return to earth from Saturn
Journey back is meant to be fast
Than the time to reach this planet
Mr. Flint had told us that
To think about it we have a week
Hope we find a way by then'

Soon a message came from earth
On the coordinates to land the craft

Which was a plain in the wild
Set apart from the outside world

It was a week since they started
Guna could see earth in front

Like a crystal blue in colour
With some green seen from afar

White clouds in a group were flying by
It was a signal of home nearby

Round and round did they go
Around the atmosphere of the earth

Clouds were on their own trip
Always in search of a perfect place

With possibility of rain and thunder
Enough for them to fall to ground

Clouds did see the spacecraft fly by
With a new guest who had come by

Guna had a plan in his mind
To rescue the sparrow at any cost

He changed the craft to a new direction
To a place far away from the men

Now they were going into the ocean
One which lay between the desert

'It is less dense at the sides'
Guna had heard it from his friends

Spacecraft nosedived into the water
A jerk was felt inside as well

It didn't drown nor did it go down
Instead it floated with a frown

Guna could see the sky above
From the place where he was now

Craft had reached the cold water
With space enough to open the door

Water was there, till their knees
As they came out of the craft

Suit could be opened, finally
Air could be breathed, happily

Earth it was, fresh and beautiful
Seeing it did make their heart full

Nothing like this will ever be seen
They did realize it by now

Guna held the sparrow close to his chest
Soon friends will come in search of craft

He walked forward on the sand
Determined to save the sparrow's life

Guna was mistaken, proved soon
The sparrow was missing from his arms

He had flown to see the land, far away
As Guna and Krishna couldn't fly

They stood watching the little sparrow
Till he disappeared, seen as a point now

By then the people had come there
In search of those, who came back

After a long time did Guna smile
People thought it was on seeing them

They didn't know about the sparrow
Who just escaped on his own

Bringing a smile on Guna's face
Also on Krishna's, who stood close

Guna and Krishna didn't wait
They did go, like Mr. Flint

Into a place far from the land
Where there were less people around

They didn't share much with anyone
On the travel that they were on

Once in a while, they did remember
About The Bird and the sparrow herd

****

One fine day, as Guna went for a walk
Beyond the lawn of his house

He did hear a familiar sound
After a year was it heard

He looked in wonder at the sky
At two sparrows that flew in air

One had skin, blue in colour
Red was the colour of her beak

It felt like she did have a ribbon
That tied her hair in a place

She flew in tandem with the one
Who had come from another planet

One with feathers brown in colour
With eyes shining like a mirror

His sound was different as before
It made it an easy guess for Guna

'Where have you been?' asked Guna
As the little sparrow flew very close

Along with the friend that he got
Who was beautiful talking a lot

A yellow beam could be seen
Coming from the sky or beyond

Was it a flash of some star
Or a search team from Saturn

Still trying to find the sparrow
Whose feathers shone in the light

He hid behind some thick bushes
As if it would make him invisible

He was not ready, to go back soon
Until he sees earth and moon

Sparrow had travelled lots of miles
Flying around many planets and skies

Just to see this beautiful place
The one with all five elements

About the Author

A Romantic delight, Story of Blue Ocean, Epics of Olga - These are the books written by Soumya P.

www.ingramcontent.com/pod-product-compliance
Lightning Source LLC
LaVergne TN
LVHW041121150826
845673LV00007B/2142

* 9 7 9 8 8 9 5 8 8 7 6 5 3 *